BULLETPROOF DIET COOKBOOK

Quick and Easy Bulletproof Diet Recipes
to Lose Weight, Feel Energized,
and Gain Radiant Health and
Optimal Focus

Madison Miller

DISCLAIMER

The content found here is for informational purpose only. It is in no way intended to be a substitute for professional medical advice or medical counselling, diagnosis, or as a treatment/cure for any disease or health condition and nor should it be construed as such. Always seek the advice of your physician or a qualified health professional before making any changes to your diet, exercise, or lifestyle or for questions regarding a specific medical condition. Never disregard professional medical advice or delay in seeking professional medical advice because of something you have read in this book.

CONTENTS

AVANT-PROPOS

Hello! My name is Madison Miller, and I am a nutritionist. I have been following a paleo diet for a few years now. I also started to follow the Dave's Asprey Bulletproof diet. I finally decided to take the plunge in June 2014, and I am so glad I did! I really feel bulletproof! It has been a tremendous journey for me. I lost about 15 pounds. I feel energized, but most of all, I feel so much more focused than before. I can truly say I have a radiant health! I decided to write this book to share a few of my own recipes that I eat on a regular basis with fellow Bulletproof dieters. I am by no mean an expert on the Bulletproof diet, but I have researched and accumulated the knowledge necessary to understand the foundations of Dave Asprey's diet. The hardest part for me at the beginning was to find and explore what my choices of meals were. I hope these recipes will give you some ideas on your Bulletproof journey.

To your health, mind and body,

Madison

INTRODUCTION

The Bulletproof Diet is the brainchild of biohacker Dave Asprey who says he initially began his own research into diet in an attempt to tackle his weight problem. He says he has spent more than two decades researching how best to fuel the body to obtain optimal physical and mental performance. I will not detail the diet in this book as this is a cookbook, but I highly suggest you read Dave Asprey's Bulletproof Diet book. It is available on Amazon or in any bookstore in the health section. It has all the information regarding the diet. Dave Asprey's website is also a MUST stop on your Bulletproof journey. It has tons of information, and it is designed to give you all the information you need regarding every aspect of the Bulletproof diet including the scientific research behind the diet and the diet roadmap. To visit the website go to http//:www.bulletproofexec.com.

Going Bulletproof is going to have you feeling like a lean, mean, kicking-ass-taking-no- prisoners-kind-of-machine. The Bulletproof Diet has taken the world by storm and for good reason, as it promises to increase mental performance and reduce weight. All this while allowing you to eat the delicious foods you love. It may sound hard to believe, but it works, and there are thousands of followers to prove it.

Going Bulletproof is going to have you feeling like a high energy machine. You will feel yourself getting lighter in body and stronger in mind. The key to going Bulletproof is forgetting about your old ideas about fat and protein. Going Bulletproof means embracing the fat and being careful to put the right amounts of protein from the right sources into your body.

This book has been designed to give the Bulletproof dieter meal options that respect the Bulletproof general guidelines. The meals have been created to ensure that you are getting the required amount of fat, protein, and carbohydrates with each dish. It is crucial that you get the right amount of nutrients so that your brain and body can function at optimal levels all the time.

Pastured eggs, and grass-fed beef and lamb are your best animal sources of protein and fat. It is these proteins that we've focused on. We've provided recipes for sous-vide eggs, one of the best ways to cook eggs so you don't lose any of the benefits but still ensure your eggs are fully cooked. You will find delicious recipes for Aromatic Beef Tenderloin, (Offal) Lamb Stew and Beefy Avocado Chili.

Good quality seafood is also a good source of heart-healthy fats, and you will find delicious recipes including Raspberry Butter Salmon. There are also delicious recipes for low-protein days like Sweet Potato Bake or Fennel and Avocado Salad. There's also a delicious selection of condiments and sides like Black Pepper Gravy and Bulletproof Fake Cheese.

Diet Breakdown

Each day will start off with Bulletproof Coffee followed by a lunch meal and a dinner meal. If you are new to Bulletproof, then you want to do some intermittent fasting. That means lunch and dinner should be eaten within 6 hours of each other, and the lunch should be eaten approximately 16 hours after the previous night's dinner. However, if you've gone through the induction phase, than you can be a little more flexible of when you eat your meals.

Your meals are going to be composed of high fat and medium levels of protein. Along with your meals, you are going to want some sort of small carbohydrate side that should be eaten shortly before your main meal or shortly after. Just remember to eat this carb within the six-hour frame if you are in the beginning of your Bulletproof plan. Also remember that although you should have some carbs, those should be limited if you are trying to lose weight.

Overall, your meals should consist of lots of veggies, a healthy source of fat, and protein. You should avoid sugars, whole grains, dairy, and processed foods.

All the produce you consume should be organic. The butter should come from grass-fed cows, the meat from pastured grass-fed animals, and wild-caught fish and seafood. In the recipes, I do not always refer to organic, but it is implicitly intended.

You are going to want to ensure you are getting an adequate amount of fat. That is why you're going to be noshing on quite a bit of grass-fed butter. You're also going to be hearing about MCT oil a lot while on the Bulletproof Diet. MCT stands for Medium Chain Triglycerides. These are fats made out of 6-10 carbon atoms per chain versus Long Chain Triglycerides which are made on average of twice as many atoms. The fact that MCT's are shorter means they are broken down much faster by the body and used for energy instead of being stored as fat. These MCT's also provide the calorie punch you need to get you through your day.

Following the overall Bulletproof plan promises to bring major changes to your life. However, remember that there are certain foods, which although healthy for some people, may be your personal nemeses. Taking an allergy test is a great way to figure out what foods are and aren't good for you. However, if this is out of your budget, you can still get to know what foods are the best for you and what foods are the worst by being particularly sensitive and aware of your own body's function when you eat different types of foods.

One crucial thing to take into consideration when changing your diet is the simple fact that you are unique and so are your body's needs. There is never a one-size-fits-all solution. Follow the overall plan, adjust it for you, and remember this is all a part of the plan to getting you Bulletproof.

PASTURED EGGS

Sous Vide Eggs and Broccoli

Overcooking food is harmful. Outside of eating foods raw, it is best to cook them over low heat in order to ensure that they don't lose their nutrients. One of the best ways to cook animal proteins while ensuring you're not overcooking is the sous vide way. Sous vide allows you to cook food at a low temperature over a longer period of time, thereby ensuring cooking/sterilization takes place while nutrients and moisture are retained.

Serves: 2
Preparation time: 10 minutes
Cooking time: 15 minutes

Ingredients
4 pastured eggs
4 cups broccoli
2 tbsp grass-fed butter
Water

Directions

1. Fill your sous vide machine with water and heat to 145°F/63°C. Place your eggs with shells into water, and cook for one hour to achieve the perfectly poached egg.

2. If you don't have a sous vide machine, you can recreate one using your oven.

3. Preheat oven to 140°F.

4. Fill an oven-safe pot with water, and bring this water up to 140°F, use a thermometer to check on water temperature.

5. Once temperature hits the required mark, add eggs.

6. Cook eggs at this temperature for one hour.

7. While eggs are cooking, heat butter in a skillet over medium heat.

8. Add broccoli and sauté for 4 minutes, sprinkle with salt, set aside.

9. Enjoy your sous vide eggs along with buttery vegetables.

Basil Green Eggs

Add a little basil to change your everyday eggs to something gourmet. The spinach gives you that iron you need and combined with the fat from your eggs and ghee, you have a meal that will keep you moving.

Serves: 4-6

Preparation time: 10 minutes

Cooking time: 20 minutes

Ingredients

4 pastured eggs

4 leaves fresh basil

4 cups spinach

4 tbsp grass fed ghee

1 lemon, juiced

1 tsp salt

Directions

1. Preheat oven to 320°F/161°C.
2. Heat ghee in cast iron skillet over medium.
3. Add basil and stir for 30 seconds so that your ghee absorbs the basil flavor.
4. Add spinach and lemon juice, sauté for 2 minutes.
5. Create four small pits in the spinach mixture, and crack one egg into each pit.

6. Stick your cast iron skillet in the oven for 30 minutes, remove, and enjoy.

Avocado Pots with Sous Vide Eggs

These little guys are like little surprises in an edible bowl. They are full of heart-healthy fats to keep you energized through a whole afternoon.

Serves: 4

Preparation time: 20 minutes

Cooking time: 20 minutes

Ingredients

4 sous vide eggs

2 avocados

4 tbsp grass-fed butter

1 tsp dried basil

½ tsp sea salt

½ tsp black pepper

Directions

1. Preheat oven to 320ºF/160ºFand line a tray with parchment.
2. Slice avocadoes in half, remove pit, and scoop out half of flesh from all halves, place flesh in blender.
3. Add basil, salt, black pepper to blender and mix.
4. Set avocado bowls on tray, pour basil mixture into each cup.

5. Place a teaspoon of butter into each cup and stick in the oven for 45 minutes.
6. Top each avocado pot with sous vide egg and serve.

Smoked Salmon and Eggs

Sometimes you need to just eat and go without getting fancy, but you still need to stick to your overall plan of only consuming that which is going to do your body good. This little dish sounds like something you might find on a fancy hotel breakfast menu, but it will take you just minutes to make and is full of good protein and good fat that's going to keep you full.

Serves: 2
Preparation time: 10 minutes
Cooking time: 10 minutes

Ingredients

4 pastured eggs, poached or sous vide method
½ cup smoked salmon
4 tbsp grass-fed ghee, melted
1 tsp dill
Salt

Directions

1. Heat ghee in skillet over medium heat, add dill, and stir for 30 seconds, remove from heat.
2. Divide equally the smoked salmon between two plates. Top with two poached eggs and drizzle with dill-infused ghee.

3. Sprinkle with a little salt, if desired.

Asparagus Noodle Soup

Eggs make a great substitute for noodles in a soup. In fact they are essentially an egg noodle without the sticky, carbohydrate-stuffed stuff. Adding eggs to otherwise vegetable-based soups is also a great way to up the fat and protein content.

Serves: 4
Preparation time: 5 minutes
Cooking time: 30 minutes

Ingredients

1 lb asparagus, trimmed
5 pastured eggs
4 cups grass-fed beef stock
2 cups coconut milk
1 tsp salt
1 tsp black pepper
2 tbsp coconut oil
½ tsp dried rosemary
1 lemon

Directions

1. Slice asparagus into 1" pieces
2. Heat coconut oil in soup pot over medium heat, add asparagus, sauté for a minute.
3. Add grass-fed beef stock coconut milk, salt, black pepper, and bring to a boil. Reduce heat medium-low, cover and let simmer for 20 minutes.
4. While the soup is simmering, whisk eggs together in bowl.

5. Uncover soup pot once 20 minutes are up. Using fork, drop small amounts of egg into soup pot.
6. Remove from heat and serve with a garnish of lemon.

GRASS-FED BEEF

Beefy Avocado Chili

This lovely, creamy chili is full of lovely fat as well as good dose of protein. The soft bites of avocado thrown in at the end help pull this chili together by providing a saucy, creamy consistency.

Serves: 6
Preparation time: 10 minutes
Cooking time: 30 minutes

Ingredients

2 lbs grass-fed beef tip

2 avocados, peeled, pitted

2 stalks, celery, chopped

1 fennel bulb, chopped

1 tsp dried oregano, cumin

½ tsp paprika

4 tbsp grass-fed ghee

4 cups organic beef stock

Salt and black pepper

Directions

1. Slice beef and avocado into ½" pieces.
2. Heat ghee in soup pot, add beef and brown for 2 minutes.
3. Add celery, fennel and sauté for another two minutes.
4. Add oregano, cumin, paprika, ½ tsp salt, ½ tsp black pepper and beef stock, bring to a boil, reduce heat to low.
5. Stir in avocado, cover, turn heat off and wait for 10 minutes before serving.

Bulletproof Meatballs

Traditional meatballs provide a great way to get your protein, and here we add that extra kicker of fat to make this a Bulletproof meal.

Serves: 4

Preparation time: 20 minutes

Cooking time: 45 minutes

Ingredients

Meatballs

1 lb lean grass-fed ground beef

1 carrot, grated

1 tsp dried coriander

1 fennel bulb, finely chopped

2 tbsp MCT oil

2 tbsp grass-fed butter, melted

1 tbsp collagen

1 tsp salt

1 tsp black pepper

Directions

1. Preheat oven to 320°F/161°C and line roasting tray with parchment. Lightly coat parchment with 2 tbsp grass-fed butter.

2. Combine ground beef with carrot, coriander, fennel, salt, black pepper, collagen, MCT oil. Mix.
3. Shape beef mixture into 1" meatballs, place on roasting tray and bake for 45 minutes, turn halfway through.

Aromatic Beef Tenderloin

Lovely spices come together to make this more than your average beef tenderloin. The high protein content of the beef is balanced with the additional fat.

Serves: 4

Preparation time: 15 minutes

Cooking time: 20 minutes

Ingredients

1 lb grass-fed beef tenderloin

3 carrots, sliced

4 cups broccoli florets

4 tbsp coconut oil

4 tbsp grass-fed butter

1 lemon, juiced

½ tsp cumin

½ tsp cinnamon, grated

½ tsp cardamom, crushed

1 tsp salt

Directions

1. Combine spices in a bowl.
2. Preheat oven to 320ºF/161ºC and line a roasting pan with parchment.
3. Rub beef tenderloin with spices, place on roasting tray.

4. Heat coconut oil and butter in cast iron skillet over medium-high heat.
5. Sear beef tenderloin on all sides, add carrots and broccoli to pan, slide into oven and cook for 45 minutes.

Thai Coconut Beef

Coconut milk is a wonderful fatty, natural replacement for creamy dairy, and since Thai recipes include a lot of coconut, this recipe makes a perfect and delicious addition to your new diet and lifestyle.

Serves: 4
Preparation time: 10 minutes
Cooking time: 20 minutes

Ingredients

1 lb grass-fed sirloin steak
5 cups broccoli florets
2 green onions, chopped
1 tbsp lemongrass, chopped
2 cups coconut milk
¼ cup coconut oil
Salt and black pepper to taste

Directions

1. Slice sirloin steak against the grain into ½" wide strips.
2. Heat coconut oil in skillet over medium heat, add steak, sprinkle with a little salt and cook for 30 seconds, turn and cook for another 30 seconds, remove to plate.

3. In same skillet, add lemongrass, onions, broccoli florets, and sauté for a minute.
4. Add coconut milk and bring to a simmer.
5. Return steak to skillet, cover, turn off heat and rest steak in coconut milk sauce for 10 minutes before serving.

Steak and Sweet Potato Skewers

There's something about eating food on a stick that just makes it a little more fun. These steak and sweet potato skewers are chock-full of vitamins and they are a whole lot delicious too.

Serve: 6
Preparation time: 10 minutes
Cooking time: 10 minutes

Ingredients
1 lb grass-fed top sirloin steak
1 medium yellow onion, quartered
1 sweet potato
1 tsp paprika
1 lime, juiced
Salt and black pepper
Coconut oil

12 wooden bamboo skewers

Directions
1. Soak bamboo skewers in cold water for 30 minutes.
2. Lightly coat grill with coconut oil and heat on high.
3. Sprinkle sirloin with ½ tsp salt and ½ tsp black pepper.
4. Slice sirloin into 1" cubes.
5. Peel and slice sweet potato into ¼" thick slices.
6. Combine salt, paprika, black pepper, lime juice, 4 tbsp melted coconut oil in bowl, add onions, sweet potatoes and coat.
7. Thread one cube, 1 piece onion, 3 slices potato, repeat on skewer, divide amongst 12 skewers.
8. Grill for approximately 8 minutes for medium, turning skewers to ensure all sides get even heat.

Bison Sirloin Steak Tacos

This is a recipe you'll want to make again and again. It's that good! It has just enough spices, and the bison gives it a special flavor perfect for a taco filling.

Serves: 4

Preparation time: 1 hour and 15 minutes

Cooking time: 15 minutes

Ingredients

1 lb grass fed bison strip loin

1 yellow onion, sliced

1 green bell pepper, sliced

4 cloves garlic, peeled and chopped

1 tsp each sea salt and black pepper

3 tbsp grass fed butter

1 avocado

8 leaves Boston Lettuce

½ tsp cumin

½ tsp oregano

½ paprika

½ tsp black pepper

1 tsp salt

2 tbsp MCT Oil

Directions

1. Combine spices, salt and MCT oil in a refrigerator bag.

2. Thinly-slice strip loin against the grain and place strips into refrigerator bag. Shake it up and refrigerate overnight or at least for an hour.

3. Heat butter in skillet over medium, add strip loin and sauté for two minutes. Remove from pan, and reserve.

4. Into same skillet add onion, bell pepper, and garlic. Sauté for two minutes, return beef to pan and sauté together for a minute.

5. To serve, lay two leaves of lettuce on a flat service plate, with half of each overlapping each other. Repeat for the other servings.

6. Slice the avocado into thin strips.

7. Spoon some of the bison mixture down the center of the overlapped leaves, opposite of where the leaves overlap. Place a few strips of avocado.

8. Wrap and enjoy!

GRASS-FED LAMB

Lamb Stew

Offal is excellent for your body, skin and hair, yet most of us don't get a lot of these parts into our diet. Some people are turned off by the taste while others by the prep. The wonderful thing about creating this lamb stew in a crockpot is that you don't have to worry too much about either. The prep is simple and the medley of flavors in the stew come together for a beautiful taste that really has nothing "offal" about it.

Serves: 4-6
Preparation time: 15 minutes
Cooking time: 8 hours

Ingredients
2 lbs grass-fed lamb heart
2 lbs grass-fed lamb liver
2 scallions, minced
3 carrots, chopped
2 celery stalks, chopped
4 cups grass-fed beef stock
2 sprigs thyme
2 sprigs rosemary

1 tsp black pepper

1 tsp sea salt

Directions

- Tie sprigs of thyme and rosemary together with butcher's twine, set aside.
- Slice lamb liver and heart into 1" cubes.
- Heat butter in skillet over medium-high heat and brown offal.
- Place scallion in the bottom of a large slow cooker, top with browned offal and add remaining ingredients including thyme, rosemary on top.
- Cook on low for 8 hours.

Curry-Spiced Lamb

The flavors of Madras are enough to bring color to blank walls or even the blank but delicious palate of buttery butter. Here we have a lovely cut of grass-fed lamb that will give you the healthy fat you need to process those ketones. This lamb has a healthy dose of spice to ensure you don't get bored of butter and stick to the bulletproof plan.

Serves: 4
Preparation time: 20 minutes
Cooking time: 30 minutes

Ingredients

1 lb grass-fed boneless lamb

1 can coconut milk

3 cups water

½ tsp cinnamon stick, ground

½ tsp ground cloves

½ tsp ground cumin

½ tsp ground turmeric

1 tsp paprika

½ tsp black pepper

1 tsp salt

1 bay leaf

5 tbsp ghee

Directions

1. Combine spices in a large sealable bag.
2. Slice lamb into 1" cubes, place cubes in the bag. Shake until well coated, and refrigerate for an hour.
3. Heat butter in a large deep skillet over medium heat. Add lamb and brown the meat on all sides.
4. Add bay leaf, stir-in coconut milk and water.
5. Reduce heat to low, cover and allow to simmer for 20 minutes.
6. Remove bay leaf before serving.

Rosemary Lamb Medallion

This simple lamb dish takes just minutes to prepare and is spiced with homey, hearty flavors. Just pop it into the oven to cook at low heat as you whip up a side to go alongside.

Serves: 4

Preparation time: 10 minutes

Cooking time: 1 hour

Ingredients

4 grass-fed lamb medallions

5 tbsp grass-fed butter

1 lemon, juiced

1 tsp oregano

1 tsp rosemary

½ tsp paprika

1 tsp salt

Directions

- Combine oregano, paprika, rosemary, salt in a bowl.
- Rub spices into lamb, wrap in saran wrap and refrigerate overnight.
- Preheat oven to 320°F/161°C and line a roasting pan with parchment.

- Melt butter an ovenproof skillet such as a cast iron over medium heat.
- Sear lamb and place skillet into oven.
- Cook for one hour.
- Serve with an item found in "Sides."

Lamb Chops in Avocado Butter

The avocado is really one of nature's most magical creations. Its creamy texture make it a lovely base to create all sorts of sauces that would otherwise require cream. Here the avocado antes up the fat quotient and brings new depth to your lamb chop.

Serves: 2
Preparation time: 15 minutes
Cooking time: 45 minutes

Ingredients

4 grass-fed lamb chops
1 avocado
6 orange segments, skin removed
6 tbsp grass-fed ghee
Salt and black pepper

Directions

- Preheat oven to 320°F/161°C and peel, pit and slice avocado.
- Place avocado in a blender along with ½ tsp salt and ½ tsp black pepper and orange segments.
- Melt butter in a cast iron skillet over medium heat.
- Place 2 tbsp of melted butter into the avocado blender and mix avocado until smooth, set aside.

- Season lamb with salt and pepper. Sear lamb in butter in an ovenproof skillet to brown the meat on both sides, about 1 minute per side.
- Pour avocado sauce over lamb chops and bake in oven for 30-40 minutes, until the lamb is cooked to your desired doneness

WILD CAUGHT FISH AND SEAFOOD

Swordfish in Rosemary Butter Sauce

Oily fish are chock full of heart healthy Omega-3 fatty acids, and that means you can enjoy succulent pieces of flavorful fish while finding comfort in the fact that they're doing your body a whole lot of good. Here we allow oily swordfish to combine with a nice rosemary butter to heighten the flavor all the while ensuring the dish is delicious and you are well-satiated for up to 6 hours.

Serves: 2
Preparation time: 10 min.
Cooking time: 15 minutes

Ingredients

2 wild caught swordfish filets
4 tbsp unsalted grass-fed butter
1 lemon
1 tsp rosemary
Salt and black pepper

Directions

- Heat 4 tbsp unsalted grass-fed butter and rosemary in a skillet over medium heat.

- Place swordfish filets down, squeeze the juice of half a lemon over the two filets and sprinkle with a little salt and pepper, cook for 4 minutes.
- Turn the fish over carefully, ensuring you don't puncture the flesh, squeeze remaining lemon juice over top and sprinkle a little more salt and pepper, cook for another 4 minutes and serve.

Salmon in Raspberry Butter

For a little twist on your everyday salmon, add raspberries to the butter for a little bit of the sweetness you may be missing. The sweet of the raspberries pairs beautifully with salty, buttery flavor of salmon.

Serves: 2
Preparation time: 5 minutes
Cooking time: 20 minutes

Ingredients:

2 wild caught salmon filets

¼ cup raspberries

6 tbsp grass-fed butter

2 tbsp fresh lemon juice

1 tsp salt

Directions

- Heat butter in skillet over medium heat, add raspberries and cook for two minutes.
- Spoon out berries into a dish.
- Place salmon filets into butter, sprinkle with butter and a little lemon juice, cook for 4 minutes.
- Turnover, sprinkle with salt and lemon juice, cook for another 4 minutes.
- Serve with buttery berries on top.

Lime Buttered Rainbow Trout

This dish is so very simple and so very delicious. When starting out on a new diet plan it's always nice to have some simple meals to whip so that the diet doesn't turn out to be a chore. The lime and butter combo here seeps into the trout and gives you full flavor while the cooking time will leave you feeling fresh and full of energy for other things – like becoming bulletproof.

Serves: 2
Preparation time: 5 minutes
Cooking time: 35 minutes

Ingredients

2 wild caught rainbow trout, cleaned, heads cut off
¼ cup freshly squeezed lime juice
1 lime, sliced
¼ cup grass-fed butter
½ tsp sea salt
½ tsp black pepper
4 fresh rosemary springs

Directions

- Heat the oven to 320°F/161°C.
- Heat butter in a large ovenproof skillet such as a cast iron, over medium-low heat.

- Add lime juice, cook for about a minute. Remove from heat.
- Add fish to the skillet. Spoon some of the butter lime juice mixture into the trout's bellies. Add 2 rosemary springs in each trout. Sprinkle with salt and pepper.
- Cover loosely with aluminum paper.
- Place in the pre-heated oven. Bake for 30-35 minutes depending on the size of each trout. The internal temperature on an instant meat thermometer should read 140°F/61°C.
- Serve with slices of lime.

Splendid Crab Cakes

Although seafood is a good way to get away from your standard protein sources, it is very important that you are sourcing good quality, and thereby non-toxic seafood. Crab meat is one of the things you have to be particularly careful about purchasing since there is more imitation crab meat than real crab meat in most grocery stores. However, as long as you find the real crab, enjoy these delicious crab cakes. The celery and dill really give them a little something extra.

Serves: 4
Preparation time: 20 minutes
Cooking time: 30 minutes

Ingredients

1 lb crab meat

1 stalk celery, finely minced

1 tsp dill

1 pastured egg

¼ cup almond meal

2 tsp MCT oil

4 tbsp grass fed ghee, melted

Directions

- Preheat oven to 320ºF/161ºC and line a baking sheet with parchment.
- Crack egg into bowl, whisk, add crabmeat, dill, celery, MCT oil, ghee and mix well.
- Shape into 2" cakes and place on baking sheet.
- Bake in oven for 1 hour, turn halfway through.

LOW-PROTEIN DAY MEALS OR SIDES

Creamy Sweet Potato Bake

Sweet potatoes are full of carbohydrates so this makes for a great meal on a low protein day. Sweet potatoes are also full of vitamins so high carb can also mean high nutrient. The coconut milk provides an extra fatty sweetness to bring together the whole dish.

Serves: 2
Preparation time: 15 minutes
Cooking time: 1hour and 5 minutes

Ingredients:

3 sweet potatoes, peeled, chopped

1 cup coconut milk

4 tbsp grass-fed butter

2 tbsp MCT oil

1 tsp salt

Directions

- Preheat oven to 320ºF/161ºC and lightly coat a 10 x 10" baking dish with butter.
- Steam sweet potatoes for 20 minutes or until tender. Place in prepared baking dish.

- Place coconut milk, grass-fed butter, MCT oil, whey protein and salt in blender and mix until smooth.
- Pour blender mixture over sweet potato and bake in the oven for 45 minutes.

Fennel and Avocado Salad

This fennel and avocado salad is quite refreshing even though it does have the fat content you need. The raw ingredients provide a healthy crispness and the lemon provides a nice cleansing kick

Serves: 2

Preparation time: 10 minutes

Cooking time: 0 minutes

Ingredients:

2 fennel bulbs,

2 carrots, grated

1 scallion, thinly-sliced

¼ cup almonds, chopped

1 avocado, pitted, peeled, diced

2 lemons, juiced

4 tbsp MCT oil

1 tsp salt

Directions

- Thinly slice fennel bulbs.
- Combine fennel with scallion, carrots, and almonds in a bowl.
- In a smaller bowl combine lemon juice, MCT oil, salt.

- Toss lemony dressing with fennel salad.
- Let rest at room temperature for 10 minutes before serving.

Cauliflower Cream Soup with Basil Drops and Bacon

This soup is very satisfying. It's silky smooth and the goodness of the bacon and basil drops just add a wonderful touch of flavour.

Serving: 6–8
Preparation time: 10 minutes
Cooking time: 30 minutes

Ingredients:

1 large cauliflower, washed and cut into small pieces

5 tablespoons coconut oil, melted

1 bunch of fresh basil leaves (about 1 cup)

6 pasture, preservative-free bacon slices

6 cups skim milk

½ cup grass-fed cream

1 yellow onion, chopped

Salt and white pepper

Directions

- Heat 1 tablespoon coconut oil in a large saucepan or soup kettle over medium-high heat. Add onion and cook for 2–3 minutes until tender and fragrant.

- Add cauliflower, stir until well coated and stir for 1 minute more. Add skim milk and cream so it almost covers the cauliflower and onions. Reduce heat to medium-low. Cook covered for 25–30 minutes until the cauliflower is very tender.
- Preheat the oven to 320°F/161°C.
- In the meantime, prepare the basil oil drops. In a small food processor or using an immersion hand-held blender, add basil leaves and remaining coconut oil, blend well, about 3–5 minutes, until the oil and basil are perfectly combined. Set aside.
- Arrange the 6 bacon slices on a baking sheet lined with parchment paper. Bake for 6–8 minutes, depending on the thickness of the bacon. Let cool. Break up each slice into pieces.
- When the cauliflower is well-cooked and tender, using an immersion hand-held blender, blend the soup until you obtain a smooth purée. If the soup is too thick for your liking, you can add some warm water and mix well until you get the desired consistency. This step can also be made using a food processor and blending the soup in 3–4 batches then putting the soup back in the saucepan or soup kettle and warming it up on low heat for a few minutes until heated through.

- Season the soup with salt and white pepper to taste.
- Before serving, add a few drops of the basil oil on top and decorate with bacon pieces.

Fennel and Dill Butter 'Rice'

Cauliflower infused with butter and dill with the pleasant bitter of fennel makes for such a delicious rice dish that you might just want to enjoy it on its own – and you can on protein fast days.

Serves: 4
Preparation time: 10 minutes
Cooking time: 10 minutes

Ingredients

1 medium cauliflower

1 fennel bulb, finely-chopped

2 tbsp dill, chopped

5 tbsp grass-fed butter

½ tsp cumin

1 tsp salt

2 cups hot water

Directions

- Stem cauliflower and grate florets into small granules.
- Heat butter, add cumin and stir for 15 seconds.
- Mix in fennel, cauliflower, salt and finally add water.

- Bring to a boil, reduce heat to low, cover and steam for 20 minutes.
- Remove pan from heat and rest for 10 minutes before uncovering.

SIDES

Jicama Fries

Jicama makes for a great potato substitute thanks to its similar consistency when cooked. Enjoy these jicama fries as a fantastic side dish or even enjoy them along with a salad on low protein days.

Serves: 2
Preparation time: 10 minutes
Cooking time: 45 minutes

Ingredients
1 Jicama
1 tsp salt
4 tbsp grass-fed butter, melted

Directions
- Preheat oven to 320°F/161°C and line a baking sheet with parchment.
- Slice jicama into ½"-wide fries.
- Toss the jicama fries with grass-fed butter, salt.
- Place fries on baking sheet in a single layer and bake for 45 minutes, turning halfway through.

Zucchini Rounds with Cashew Parm

Cashews provide fat as well as a taste and consistency similar to cheese. We've created a zucchini bake with this cashew-inspired Parm for a little Italian in your life.

Serves: 2
Preparation time: 5 minutes
Cooking time: 20 minutes

Ingredients:

4 medium zucchinis

¼ cup cashews, crushed

½ lemon, juiced

1 tsp salt

1 tbsp oregano

4 tbsp grass-fed butter, melted

Directions

- Preheat oven to 320°F/161°C and line a baking sheet with parchment.
- Slice zucchini into ½"-thick rounds.
- Mix cashews with salt, oregano, lemon juice and melted butter.

- Pour mixture over zucchini and bake in oven for 35 minutes.
- Enjoy with dinner or increase the helping for protein fast days.

Brussels Sprouts and Bacon

Yes, it is true that bacon does make everything better, especially for those of you who have childhood nightmares of Brussels Sprout force feedings. Brussels sprouts are a hearty vegetable. Combined with buttery bacon and buttery butter, it should have you well-satiated and full of energy

Serves: 4

Preparation time: 10 minutes

Cooking time: 16 minutes

Ingredients

16 slices pasture, preservative-free bacon

8 cups Brussels sprouts, halved

2 tbsp unsalted grass-fed butter

Directions

- Preheat oven to 350°F/177°C and line a roasting tray with aluminum foil.
- Place bacon slices on roasting tray along with Brussels sprouts and into the oven for 12 minutes.
- Remove from heat, chop bacon slices into quarters.

- Heat butter in a skillet over medium heat, add Brussels sprouts and sauté for a minute, add bacon slices and sauté for another 2 minutes.
- Serve hot.

Radish in Dill Butter Sauce

Radishes are great detoxing agents and in turn are a nice addition to any meal. They're also a good source of potassium, and paired with Dill Butter, make for sweet and savory side dish.

Serves: 2
Preparation time: 5 minutes
Cooking time: 5-7 minutes

Ingredients:

8 red radish, stemmed

5 tbsp grass fed butter

2 tbsp dill, chopped

1 tsp salt

Directions

- Slice radish into thin slices (as thin as you can get them).
- Melt butter in skillet over medium heat along with rosemary.
- Add radish to butter and sauté for 5-7 minutes or until tender.
- Remove from heat and serve along with your dinner meal.

Carrot Sauté

Carrots are full of wonderful anti-oxidants, and they also give you a little bit of that sweetness you may be craving while getting bulletproof.

Serves: 4
Preparation time: 10 minutes
Cooking time: 10 minutes

Ingredients:

4 cups carrots, grated

2 tbsp coconut oil

4 tbsp grass-fed butter

½ cup cashews, soaked overnight

½ cup water

1 tsp lemon juice

1 tsp salt

Directions

- Heat butter and coconut oil in skillet over medium heat.
- Once melted, add carrots, sauté.
- Add lemon juice, cashews, ½ cup water, reduce heat to low, cover for 10 minutes.

BF Cauliflower Rice

This is an absolutely simple way to make rice that gives you enough rice so you get your starch fix, while the cauliflower gives your veggies and has the consistency of rice so that you feel as though you're eating more rice than you actually are.

Serves: 4
Preparation time: 10 minutes
Cooking time: 10 minutes

Ingredients

½ cup white rice
½ medium cauliflower
4 tbsp grass-fed ghee
1 tsp salt
2 cups hot water

Directions

- Grate cauliflower so you have small rice-like granules. You can also use a food processor for this step.Heat ghee in skillet over medium heat. Add rice and sauté for 30 seconds.
- Add cauliflower, salt, water and bring to a boil.
- Reduce heat to low and cook for 20 minutes.

- Turn off heat and leave covered for another 20 minutes.

CONDIMENTS

Bulletproof Fake Cheese

Here is a way to enjoy delicious cheesy flavor while avoiding dairy and getting a healthy dose of veggies. Yes, it does sound too good to be true. This cheese is made out of the goodness of zucchini with the added tart of a little lemon juice to bring out the cheesy flavor.

Serves: 6
Preparation time: 10 minutes
Cooking time: 20 minutes

Ingredients:
4 zucchinis, peeled
1 tbsp MCT oil
½ lemon, juiced
2 tbsp grass-fed butter
2 tbsp agar powder
½ tsp salt

Directions
- Coat a 10 x 10" dish with a little grass-fed butter, set aside.

- Thinly slice peeled zucchini and steam for 20 minutes.
- Place steamed zucchini in a blender with MCT oil, grass-fed butter, lemon juice, agar powder and salt, mix until smooth.
- Scoop zucchini blend into dish, cover and refrigerate overnight.
- Use as a condiment with meats or amp up the quantity and make it a star on your protein-fast days.

Not Your Mediterranean Neighbor's Hummus

Hummus is delightful not just for the earthy taste but also for that buttery consistency that just exudes richness. Legumes are a no-go if you truly want to be bulletproof, so we've whipped up this concoction that does hummus the way the chick pea once did.

Serves: 4
Preparation time: 10 minutes
Cooking time: 15 minutes

Ingredients:

4 cups cauliflower florets

½ cup cashews, soaked overnight

½ lemon juiced

½ tsp paprika

1 tsp salt

4 tbsp grass-fed butter

1 cup water

Directions

- Bring cup of water to a boil, add cauliflower florets, and turn heat to low, cover for 10 minutes.

- Place cauliflower florets, cashew, lemon juice, paprika, grass-fed butter and salt in a blender, mix until fairly smooth (it is ok if it's a little grainy like hummus made from chick peas).
- Serve as a dip with cut vegetables such as celery, carrot, cauliflower, and broccoli.

Dill Sauce

Dill is one of those herbs that manages to kick up any dish. So enjoy this sauce with meats, fish, or veggies for an ante-up on flavor.

Serves: 2

Prep Time: 15 minutes.

Cooking time: 0 minutes

Ingredients

2 pastured eggs

½ cup grass-fed ghee, melted

½ lemon, juiced

2 tbsp fresh dill, chopped

¼ tsp dry mustard

½ tsp sea salt

Directions

- Crack eggs into blender, mix until combined.
- Slowly pour ghee into blender while mixing on low, add dry mustard, sea salt.
- Remove sauce into bowl, mix in dill, refrigerate for an hour before serving.

Bacon Hollandaise

Creamy hollandaise sauce just got a whole lot tastier with the simple addition of bacon. Bacon isn't one of your top fat and protein sources, so it is best to limit its consumption. However, enjoying a little Bacon Hollandaise with some veggies is just fine once in a while.

Serves: 4
Preparation time: 10 minutes
Cooking time: 5 minutes

Ingredients

4 pastured egg yolks
¼ cup cooked, chopped pasture, preservative-free bacon
1 cup unsalted grass-fed butter
2 tsp lemon juice
2 tsp MCT oil

Directions

- Melt butter in a saucepan.
- Place egg yolks in blender and mix until blended, slowly add in melted butter while continually mixing on low speed.

- Pour lemon juice and blend until just mixed. Pour into serving dish.
- Stir in chopped bacon.
- Allow flavors to blend for 20 minutes before serving.

Black Pepper Gravy

Enjoy this gravy with any one of the meat dishes in this book for a dose of extra fat and flavor.

Serves: 4

Preparation time: 10 minutes

Cooking time: 5 minutes

Ingredients

1 stalk celery, quartered

1 carrot, quartered

1 tsp rosemary

6 tbsp grass-fed butter

1 tsp cracked black pepper

½ tsp salt

1 bay leaf

1 cup water

Directions

- Heat butter into skillet over medium heat.
- Add celery, carrot in butter and sauté for five minutes.
- Add remaining ingredients, bring to a boil, cover and remove from heat.
- After 15 minutes uncover dish, remove veggies and bay leaf and serve.

SMOOTHIE RECIPES

Coconut Coffee Latte Smoothie

And this is how the magic happens. A frothy cup of freshly-brewed, toxin-free coffee mixed with creamy butter and a few drops of body-boosting MCT oil, and you are ready to ride through this morning like a superstar.

Serves: 2

Preparation time: 5 minutes

Ingredients

1 cup brewed Upgraded Coffee

1 tbsp organic wheatgrass juice

¾ cup canned coconut milk

4 tbsp grass-fed butter

2 tbsp Upgraded Whey Protein

2 tbsp MCT oil

2 tsp xylitol

Directions

- Combine ingredients in blender and mix until smooth.

Buttery Vanilla Bean Latte

For a hearty start to your day sans the coffee but with the fat or even as a quick meal replacement if required, whip up this delicious latte that offers up a full dose of healthy fat from grass-fed butter, coconut milk, and MCT oil.

Serves: 2

Preparation time: 10 minutes

Ingredients

2 pastured egg yolks

¾ cup canned coconut milk

½ cup filtered water

2 tbsp MCT oil

4 tbsp grass fed butter

2 tsp Stevia

1 tsp Upgraded Vanilla Powder

Directions

- Bring your water and coconut milk to a boil, remove from heat.
- Pour hot mixture along with MCT oil into blender, add the crushed vanilla bean and Stevia, mix until frothy.

Chocolate Bulletproof Smoothie

Sometimes you want a change from the everyday and as much as you love your Bulletproof coffee, you might just want to give it a flavor kick. Here we add all-natural cacao for a chocolaty twist to your morning buzz.

Serve: 2

Preparation time: 5 minutes

Ingredients

1 cup Upgraded Coffee, cooled

2 pastured eggs

4 tbsp grass-fed butter

½ avocado, pitted, peeled, chopped

2 tbsp Upgraded Chocolate Powder

½ cup ice

Directions

- Place coffee in blender along with remaining ingredients, mix until smooth.

Eggstra Energy Shake

This is a super-powered smoothie that will keep you full for at least 6 hours and even longer if you aren't very active during that time period.

Serves: 2

Preparation time: 5 minutes

Ingredients

½ cup organic coffee

2 pastured egg yolks

1 pastured egg

4 tbsp grass-fed butter

¾ cup canned coconut milk

2 tsp xylitol

¼ cup ice

Directions

- Combine ingredients in blender and mix.

Matcha Antioxidant Smoothie

Known as green tea's superior sibling, Matcha tea is a powerful source of antioxidants, vitamins, and minerals. The tea strength lies in its use of the whole tea leaf, allowing you to get the benefits of a whole lot of green tea in just a cup. The tea makes for a perfect mix with Bulletproof ingredients

Serves: 1

Preparation time: 5 minutes

Ingredients

1 cup Matcha green tea

2 tbsp grass fed butter

1 tbsp Krill Oil

¼ cup canned coconut milk

1 tbsp Upgraded Vanilla Powder

2 tsp Stevia

Directions

- Combine ingredients in blender and mix.

Collagen Matcha Smoothie

Adding collagen protein to your smoothie takes this drink from fantastic to body-shifting. Your body needs collagen for essential functions like repair and maintenance. It also helps your joints to glide as smooth as silk.

Serves: 2

Preparation time: 5 minutes

Ingredients

1 cup Matcha green tea

4 tbsp grass fed butter

½ cup canned coconut milk

2 tbsp Upgraded Collagen Protein

2 tsp xylitol

½ cup ice

Directions

- Combine ingredients in blender and mix.

Kale Smoothie

Delicious, healthy kale is a superfood. Given its fantastic nutritious content, it is an integral part of a healthy lifestyle. You want to steam your kale to destroy dangerous oxalate content. Kale smoothies are a great way to include this green bomb of good into your diet. The first one here is a simple Kale smoothie that will get you going in the morning with all of the Vitamin A and K you're going to need.

Serves: 2
Preparation time: 5 minutes

Ingredients

½ cup steamed kale

2 tbsp collagen protein

4 tbsp grass fed butter

2 tsp MCT Oil

½ cup canned coconut milk

2 tsp Stevia

½ cup ice

Directions

- Combine ingredients in blender and mix until smooth.

Silky Smoothie

The kale and avocado combination make this drink great for an on-the-go lunch. The ginger provides an extra flavor balance that actually makes you feel that you are in fact having a meal and not a drink.

Serves: 2

Preparation time: 5 minutes

Ingredients

½ cup organic kale steamed

1 tbsp ginger, peeled, chopped

½ organic avocado, peeled, pitted, chopped

1 cup canned coconut milk

2 tsp Stevia

4 tbsp MCT oil

Directions

- Boil water, add kale, cover, and turn off heat.
- Allow steam to soften kale for 10 minutes.
- Place kale, avocado, MCT oil, 2 tsp Stevia, and coconut milk in blender and mix until smooth.

Kale and Spinach Powerhouse Smoothie

These two green veggies are the envy of the vegetable kingdom. When combined, they will make you feel like you can take on the world. Not only is spinach full of vitamins, but it is also a great source of protein. It also provides you with plenty of potassium, which is especially great for those that have given up bananas due to Bulletproof diet restrictions.

Serves: 2

Preparation time: 5 minutes

Ingredients

¼ cup steamed kale

¼ cup steamed spinach

¼ organic avocado, pitted, peeled

2 pastured egg yolks

4 tbsp grass fed butter

½ cup ice

½ tsp Himalayan pink salt

Directions

- Combine ingredients in blender and mix until smooth.

Kale-berry Smoothie

Steaming your kale is a great way to help your body more easily grab the kale nutrients. Here we have a powerhouse of antioxidants and nutrients thanks to the combination of blueberries and kale. This smoothie is going to make you feel a whole lot of strong.

Serves: 2

Preparation time: 5 minutes

Ingredients

½ cup steamed kale

½ cup blueberries

¾ cup canned coconut milk

4 tbsp grass fed butter

2 tsp Stevia

½ cup ice

Directions

- Combine ingredients in blender and mix until smooth.

Kale Lunch Smoothie

Maybe you're fasting, or maybe you just want to make a quick go of lunch. Either way, you can't go wrong with this terrific combination of kale and carrot in a cup. Carrots provide betaprotein, which can help the body fight off free radicals and keep cells healthy.

Serves: 2

Preparation time: 5 minutes

Ingredients

½ cup steamed organic kale

½ cup organic carrot juice

¼ cup organic flat-leaf parsley

4 tbsp grass fed butter

2 tbsp Brain Octane

2 tbsp Upgraded whey protein

¾ cup ice

½ tsp sea salt

Directions

- Combine ingredients in blender and mix until smooth.

Brussels Sprouts Oh My Smoothie

Erase those childhood fears! Brussels sprouts are your friends and they are amped up with a whole lot of protein and vitamins to win you over in this smoothie.

Serves: 2
Preparation time: 5 minutes

Ingredients

6 Brussels sprouts

2 pastured eggs

2 pastured egg yolks

4 tbsp grass-fed butter

2 tbsp Krill oil

¾ cup ice

Directions

- Combine ingredients in blender and mix until smooth.

Celery Burst Smoothie

Due to its high water content, celery is sometimes considered as more of a flavor addition rather than a source of any significant nutrients. However, this watery veggie is full of a host of antioxidants that help your body stay healthy. Additionally, the celery is a sturdy vegetable that lasts from 5-7 days while holding on to a large chunk of its nutrients.

Serves: 2

Preparation time: 5 minutes

Ingredients

1 celery stalk

¼ cup cooked kale

¼ cup cilantro

2 tbsp Upgraded Whey Protein

2 tbsp Brain Octane

2 tbsp apple cider vinegar

1 cup ice

1 tsp Himalayan pink salt

½ tsp oregano

Directions

- Place all ingredients in a blender and mix until smooth.

Carrot Ginger Smoothie

Carrots make a delicious and healthy addition to your smoothie and are a great source of vitamins A and C. They also provide potassium and biotin, and on top of that are a good source of natural sugar.

Serves: 2

Preparation time: 5 minutes

Ingredients

1 organic carrot, peeled, chopped

1 tbsp ginger, peeled, chopped

2 pastured eggs

4 tbsp grass fed butter

¾ cup canned coconut milk

½ tsp grated cinnamon stick

¾ cup ice

2 tsp xylitol

Directions

- Place ingredients in blender and mix until smooth.

Carrot Fresh Smoothie

The refreshing ingredients and resulting flavors in this smoothie are a wonderful to wake up to in the morning or for an afternoon pick-me-up.

Serves: 2

Preparation time: 5 minutes

Ingredients

1 carrot, peeled, chopped

1 cucumber, peeled sliced

2 tbsp spirulina

1 tbsp ginger, peeled, chopped

2 tbsp Upgraded Whey Powder

2 tsp Stevia

4 tbsp MCT oil

2 tbsp Brain Octane

1 cup water

Directions

- Place ingredients in blender and mix well.

Wheatgrass Smoothie

Wheatgrass is an amazing ingredient to add to smoothies. It blends in well and provides you with a burst of vitamins A and C as well as an ample amount of B vitamins that can be hard to come by.

Serves: 2

Preparation time: 5 minutes

Ingredients

2 tbsp wheatgrass juice

½ organic avocado, pitted, peeled

1 organic lime, juiced

4 tbsp MCT oil

2 tbsp Brain Octane

3 tbsp Upgraded Collagen Protein

½ tsp sea salt

Directions

- Place ingredients in blender and mix until smooth.

Bok Choy Blast off

This smoothie is a meal substitute with its soup-like attitude. You have plenty of vitamins and minerals from the bok choy and wheatgrass, plus the fatty inserts make sure you are satiated.

Serves: 2

Preparation time: 5 minutes

Ingredients

1 cup bok choy

1 tbsp wheatgrass juice

2 pastured egg yolks

½ avocado, pitted, peeled

4 tbsp grass fed butter

2 tbsp MCT oil

2 tbsp apple cider vinegar

Directions

- Combine ingredients in blender and mix until smooth.

Radish Smoothie

Consuming radishes is a great way to keep your system regular and clean. The carbohydrates in radishes cannot be digested and ultimately this is a good thing. These carbs help alleviate constipation, and in turn radishes can help to detoxify your body.

Serves: 2
Preparation time: 5 minutes

Ingredients

½ cup radishes, peeled, stemmed

1 lime, juiced

2 tbsp whey protein

4 tbsp MCT oil

2 tbsp Brain Octane

½ cup ice

½ cup water

½ tsp sea salt

Directions

- Place all ingredients in a blender and mix until smooth.

Squash Smoothie

The humble squash is not just for soups. You can take this big guy and all of its lovely vitamins and proteins and add it to your smoothie for a quick and delicious drinkable meal.

Serves: 2

Preparation time: 10 minutes

Ingredients

¾ cup steamed summer squash

½ cup canned coconut milk

4 tbsp butter

2 tbsp Brain Octane

2 tbsp Upgraded Whey Protein

1 tbsp ginger, peeled, chopped

½ cup ice

¼ cup water

Directions

• Place ingredients in blender and mix until smooth.

Super Matcha Smoothie

Here we take your Match tea and give it superpowers with the addition of kale. You're going to take this day by storm, pounding the pavement while on a Matcha mix high.

Serves: 2
Preparation time: 5 minutes

Ingredients

½ cup Matcha green tea

½ cup steamed organic kale

1 tsp spirulina powder

4 tbsp grass-fed butter

2 tbsp Brain Octane

1 cup ice

2 tsp xylitol

Directions

- Combine ingredients in blender and mix.

Bulletproof in Hawaii Smoothie

This smoothie is a holiday in a glass, except that you're not on holiday. You are seriously injecting super power into your body with grass fed butter, avocado, and coconut milk. The flavor kickers are the ginger and pineapple, which take the whole thing to new heights.

Serves: 2

Preparation time: 10 min.

Ingredients

1 tbsp ginger, peeled

¼ cup organic pineapple (fresh or frozen)

½ organic avocado, pitted, peeled

4 tbsp grass-fed butter

2 tbsp MCT oil

½ cup canned coconut milk

½ cup ice

2 tsp xylitol

Directions

- Combine ingredients in blender and mix until smooth.

Cocoa Tangerine Smoothie

Chocolate and orange make for a delicious combination in this smoothie. Did you know that cacao is a natural mood booster? This smoothie can double down in dessert fashion too.

Serves: 2

Preparation time: 5 minutes

Ingredients

1 organic tangerine

¾ cup canned coconut milk

2 tbsp Upgraded Chocolate Powder

2 tbsp Upgraded Whey Protein

4 tbsp grass fed butter

2 tbsp Krill Oil

1 cup ice

Directions

- Place ingredients in blender and mix.

Strawberry Smoothie

Strawberries are full of antioxidants and are, of course, delicious. This natural sugar smoothie will help you move past your sugar cravings and get on with making your body bullet proof.

Serves: 2

Preparation time: 10 minutes

Ingredients

½ organic avocado, pitted, peeled

6 organic strawberries (fresh or frozen)

¾ cup canned coconut milk

4 tbsp grass fed butter

2 tbsp Upgraded Collagen Protein

¾ cup ice cubes

Directions

- Place ingredients in blender and mix.

Basil Blueberry Smoothie

Boom! That's how this basil is going to feel first thing in the morning. Wake up with this amazing combo of basil, blueberries, and coconut milk, mixed with the oh-so goodness of creamy grass fed butter.

Serves: 2

Preparation time: 5 minutes

Ingredients

¼ cup fresh basil

½ cup organic blueberries

¾ cup canned coconut milk

4 tbsp grass fed butter

2 tbsp Brain Octane

2 tbsp Upgraded Collagen Protein

½ cup ice

Directions

- Combine ingredients in blender and mix until smooth.

Ginger Orange Smoothie

Ginger is a natural soother for the stomach. This ginger/orange combination makes for a delicious smoothie that will help you power through an afternoon.

Serves: 2

Preparation time: 5 minutes

Ingredients

1 tbsp ginger, peeled, grated

1 organic tangerine

2 pastured eggs

¾ cup canned coconut milk

4 tbsp grass fed butter

2 tbsp Krill oil

½ cup ice

Directions

1. Combine ingredients in blender and mix until smooth.

Coconut Strawberry Smoothie

Enjoy this delicious smoothie as a morning wake-me-up. The avocado and strawberry make for a smooth pink combo that will have your skin emitting a healthy glow.

Serves: 2
Preparation time: 5 minutes

Ingredients

6 organic strawberries

½ organic avocado, pitted, peeled

1 cup coconut milk

4 tbsp grass-fed butter

3 tbsp Upgraded Brain Octane

2 tbsp Upgraded Collagen Protein

2 tsp xylitol

½ cup ice

Directions

- Combine in blender and mix until smooth.

Raspberry Chocolate Smoothie

Berries provide you with all those antioxidants you need while the whey protein gives you your dose of protein combined with that nice chocolaty flavor for a good-for-you smoothie that tastes like a dessert.

Serves: 2

Preparation time: 5 minutes

Ingredients

¼ cup organic raspberries

2 tbsp Upgraded Whey Protein

¾ cup canned coconut milk

2 pastured eggs

4 tbsp grass fed butter

2 tbsp Krill oil

¾ cup ice

2 tbsp Upgraded Chocolate Powder

Directions

- Combine ingredients in blender and mix until smooth.

Blackberry Coconut Smoothie

Blackberries are a good source of fiber as well as vitamins like K and A. If you are trying to reduce your cholesterol count, they make for a great addition to your diet.

Serves: 2
Preparation time: 5 minutes

Ingredients

¼ cup organic blackberries

¾ cup canned coconut milk

4 tbsp grass-fed butter

2 tbsp Upgraded Collagen Protein

2 tbsp MCT oil

¾ cup ice

Directions

- Place ingredients in blender and mix until smooth.

Raspberry Vanilla SBP Smoothie

Raspberries are a great source of inflammatory agents and are also high in antioxidants. They also provide a healthy dose of potassium. And of course we know that while raspberries and vanilla make for the perfect flavor combination, the addition of a cucumber provides a nourished liquid source that provides a fresh flavor pop

Serves: 2

Preparation time: 5 minutes

Ingredients

¼ cup organic raspberries

1 cucumber, peeled, sliced

2 tbsp Upgraded Whey Powder

¾ cup canned coconut milk

2 tbsp MCT oil

4 tbsp ghee

1 tbsp Upgraded Vanilla Powder

½ cup ice

Directions

- Combine ingredients in blender and mix.

Goji Smoothie

Goji berries are a common ingredient in Asian medicine and have recently gained popularity in the West. They provide numerous health benefits like an immune system boost and also improve circulation.

Serves: 2

Preparation time: 5 minutes

Ingredients

2 tbsp organic Goji berries

¼ cup organic blueberries

1 tbsp wheatgrass juice

¼ cup steamed organic spinach

4 tbsp grass fed butter

2 tbsp Brain Octane

3 tbsp Upgraded Whey Protein

½ cup canned coconut milk

½ cup ice

Directions:

- Place ingredients into blender and mix until smooth.

Cashew Smoothie

The heart-healthy fats in this smoothie will really get you through the morning and well into the afternoon if you are so inclined. The spirulina provides an additional immune boost for a truly well-rounded drink.

Serves: 2

Preparation time: 5 minutes

Ingredients

¼ cup cashews

2 tbsp MCT oil

½ cup canned coconut milk

4 tbsp grass fed butter

3 tbsp Upgraded Collagen Protein

½ cup Upgraded Coffee

1 tbsp spirulina

Directions

- Combine ingredients in blender and mix until smooth.

Vanilla Almond Smoothie

Almonds are nature's gift to us. They are fatty, hearty, and great for the body and brain. The combination of honey and almonds is a wonderful match for healthy and delicious.

Serves: 2

Preparation time: 5 minutes

Ingredients

¼ cup almonds

2 tbsp Upgraded Whey Protein

2 pastured eggs

3 tbsp grass-fed butter

1 cup canned almond milk

½ up ice

2 tsp Stevia

Directions

- Combine ingredients in blender and mix until smooth.

Pecan Avocado Smoothie

Pecans are a fantastic source of vitamin E as well as a host of B-complex vitamins. Pecans belong to the Bulletproof group of nuts and provide a wonderfully delicious source of energy. Pecans also give this rich smoothie a sweet woody flavor that is reminiscent of caramel.

Serves: 2

Preparation time: 5 minutes

Ingredients

¼ cup pecans

½ avocado, pitted, peeled

¾ cup canned coconut milk

4 tbsp grass fed butter

2 tbsp MCT oil

2 tbsp Upgraded Collagen Protein

1 tbsp Upgraded Vanilla Powder

Directions

- Combine ingredients in blender and mix until smooth.

Mint Chocolate Smoothie

And to round it all off is this glass full of deliciousness and nutritious-ness. Coconut milk and MCT oil are boosting your brain to new levels while the mint and cacao powder please your palate. Creating a mind and body that is Bulletproof just got a whole lot easier and certainly tastier.

Serves: 2
Prep Time: 5 minutes.

Ingredients
¼ cup mint

1 small cucumber, peeled, chopped

2 tbsp raw cacao powder

¾ cup canned coconut milk

4 tbsp MCT oil

2 tbsp krill oil

½ cup ice

2 tsp xylitol

Directions
- Place ingredients in blender and mix until smooth.

CONCLUSION

If you've experimented with the recipes, you will have figured out that they give you major energy, remove any sign of brain fog you may have had, and all in all make you feel tremendous.

Eating the Bulletproof way is about optimizing your body so that it functions to give you the best life. It is natural to consume fats and proteins and also natural to stay away from processed foods that just keep your system plugged.

The key to following this diet is figuring out the best combination of foods that suit your body. Once you've created your perfect fuel, you are going to wake up feeling like you are ready to take on anything and everything.

And that's what it means to Bulletproof!

Other books from Madison Miller

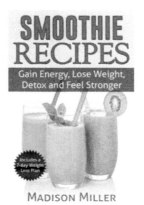

Printed in Great Britain
by Amazon